68378345R00057

Made in the USA
Columbia, SC
07 August 2019